Instant
Habitat
Dioramas

12 Super-Cool, Easy 3-D Paper Models
With Companion Observation Sheets That Teach About
Polar Regions, Rain Forests, Oceans & More

by Donald M. Silver and Patricia J. Wynne

SCHOLASTIC
PROFESSIONAL BOOKS

NEW YORK • TORONTO • LONDON • AUCKLAND • SYDNEY
MEXICO CITY • NEW DELHI • HONG KONG • BUENOS AIRES

Cover design by Pamela Simmons
Cover photograph by Donnelly Marks
Interior design by Susan Kass
Interior illustrations by Patricia J. Wynne

ISBN 0-439-04088-4
Copyright © 2001 by Donald M. Silver and Patricia J. Wynne
All rights reserved.
Printed in the U.S.A.

Table of Contents

Introduction

One of the basic science concepts taught in primary grades is that a *habitat* is the place where a group of plants and animals naturally live together. The dioramas in this book will introduce your students to various habitats—from their very own backyard to distant polar regions—and the living things that thrive in them.

As an added bonus, each back-to-back diorama will teach your students about opposites in the natural world. For example, they will see what animals in a park do in the day and at night, how living conditions differ in the front of a cave from its back, and how a forest changes in the spring and autumn.

The dioramas are easy to assemble and come with cut-out illustrations for students to enhance the habitats. (See right.) The worksheet for each diorama indicates where each cut-out piece belongs. In addition, the dioramas make attractive, 3-D classroom displays—a nice alternative to standard bulletin boards or wall hangings.

For each diorama, you will find:
- science background information
- a mini-lesson to help you teach with the diorama
- an extension activity
- book links
- a worksheet with comprehension questions for students to answer with the help of their dioramas.

How to Make the Dioramas

1. Each diorama comes with three reproducible sheets: a background showing the habitat, the foregrounds and cut-out illustrations, and a worksheet. Photocopy the three sheets for each student or small group.

2. Hold up a worksheet and show students how the border identifies each living thing in the diorama. Children can refer to the border to figure out in which side of the diorama the foregrounds and cut-out pieces belong.

3. Provide crayons and markers for students to color the illustrations.

4. Have students cut off the white border on the background page and fold the sheet in half along the dashed line. Have them cut out the two foreground pieces as well.

5. On one side of the diorama, have students tape the left side of the matching foreground piece to the diorama, as shown. Then tape the right side of the foreground to the diorama.

6. Turn the diorama around and repeat step 5 with the other foreground. The completed back-to-back diorama will stand as shown.*

7. Help children cut out the animal and/or plant pieces. Have them decide where in the diorama each piece belongs and glue or tape it in place. Tell students that they can attach the cutouts to the background or foreground. They can also have some animals extend off the edges to give the diorama a 3-D effect.

*To make some dioramas stand up better, you may want to add one piece of tape to the center of each foreground, sticking it to the background as shown. Then pinch or fold the foreground on both sides of the tape so the foreground sticks out more.

Backyard
Above and Below

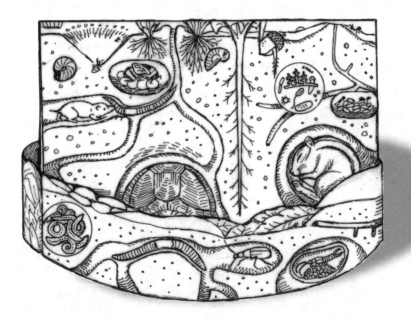

Teaching with the Diorama

1. Invite students to think about a backyard. Ask, "What kinds of plants grow there? Do any animals live in a backyard? What do they do there?" Next, have students try to imagine what goes on *below* the backyard. Have them picture plant roots, insects, such as beetles, or burrowing animals, such as shrews or moles.

2. Have students assemble their Above and Below dioramas, which feature a typical backyard. (See page 4.)

3. Ask students to look at the Above side of the diorama. Ask, "Where do you think backyard animals find food and water?" *(Many animals feed on plants, while some may feed on other animals. Water from rain may collect in puddles, from which*

SCIENCE BACKGROUND

A backyard is home to many living things—some live above ground, while others dwell below. Plants straddle both sides, with roots reaching underground to absorb water and nutrients from the soil, while stems stretch to the sky so leaves can take in sunlight and carbon dioxide to make their own food through *photosynthesis*.

Many creatures that live above ground, such as bees, grasshoppers, and butterflies, feed on plants to survive. Some animals prey on other animals. To stay safe, animals, such as chipmunks and box turtles, burrow below ground where they sleep, hide, or store food.

Book Links

One Small Square: Backyard
by Donald M. Silver and
Patricia J. Wynne
(McGraw-Hill, 1997)

Incredible Plants
by Barbara Taylor
(Firefly Books, 1996)

A Seed Grows
by Pamela Hickman
(Kids Can Press, 1997)

Answers
1. Above ground
2. Below ground
3. An earthworm
4. Eat it
5. Four
6. Below ground
7. Above ground
8. Dandelion root
9. Animals such as earthworms, shrews, or chipmunks
10. Answers will vary.

animals can drink. Some animals get water from plants.)

4. Turn to the Below side of the diorama, which shows the top layer of soil. Ask, "How is this underground habitat different from the one above ground?" *(There's no light and very little open space underground.)* Explain that earthworms, ants, moles, and other soil animals tunnel below ground, loosening and mixing topsoil. This creates spaces for air and water to reach roots and animals that live below ground.

5. Challenge students to use their dioramas to answer the questions on page 7.

Explore More!

What lives in soil?

To find out, collect about a quart of soil from outdoors and put it in a colander. Line the bottom of a glass bowl with a wet paper towel, then set the colander on the bowl. Put the bowl and colander under a lamp with the light bulb about 6 inches above the soil. Leave the light on overnight. The next day, lift the colander and invite students to look in the bowl. Offer hand lenses if necessary. Do they see any soil animals? What kind? How many? Return the soil and its animals outside after you and your students have finished observing them.

Above and Below

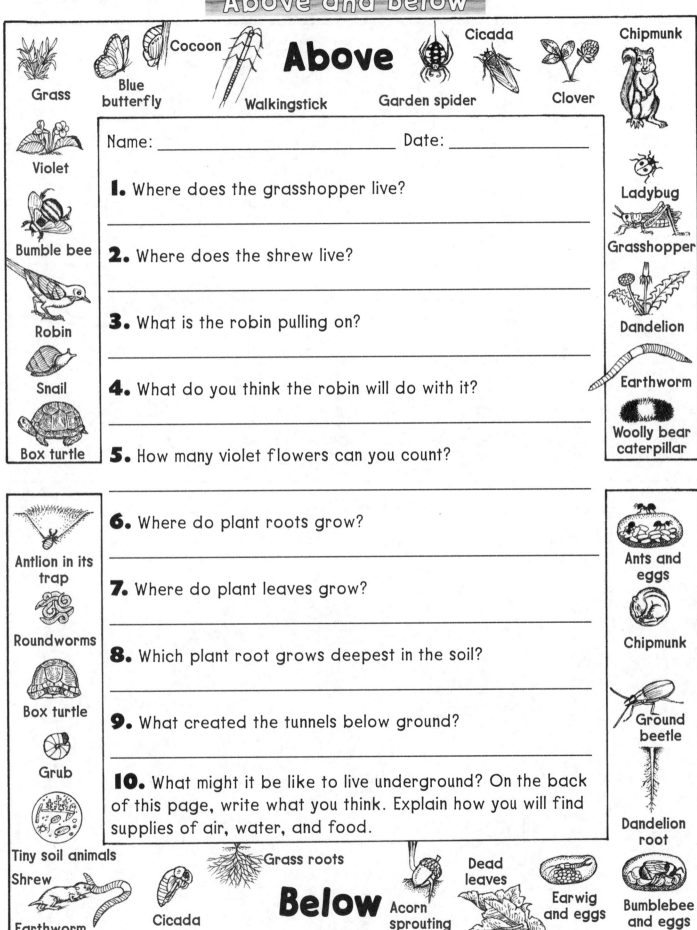

Above

Grass
Blue butterfly
Cocoon
Walkingstick
Garden spider
Cicada
Clover
Chipmunk
Violet
Bumble bee
Robin
Snail
Box turtle
Ladybug
Grasshopper
Dandelion
Earthworm
Woolly bear caterpillar

Name: _____ Date: _____

1. Where does the grasshopper live?
_____

2. Where does the shrew live?
_____

3. What is the robin pulling on?
_____

4. What do you think the robin will do with it?
_____

5. How many violet flowers can you count?

6. Where do plant roots grow?
_____

7. Where do plant leaves grow?
_____

8. Which plant root grows deepest in the soil?
_____

9. What created the tunnels below ground?
_____

10. What might it be like to live underground? On the back of this page, write what you think. Explain how you will find supplies of air, water, and food.

Antlion in its trap
Roundworms
Box turtle
Grub
Tiny soil animals
Ants and eggs
Chipmunk
Ground beetle
Dandelion root

Shrew
Earthworm
Cicada
Below
Acorn sprouting
Grass roots
Dead leaves
Earwig and eggs
Bumblebee and eggs

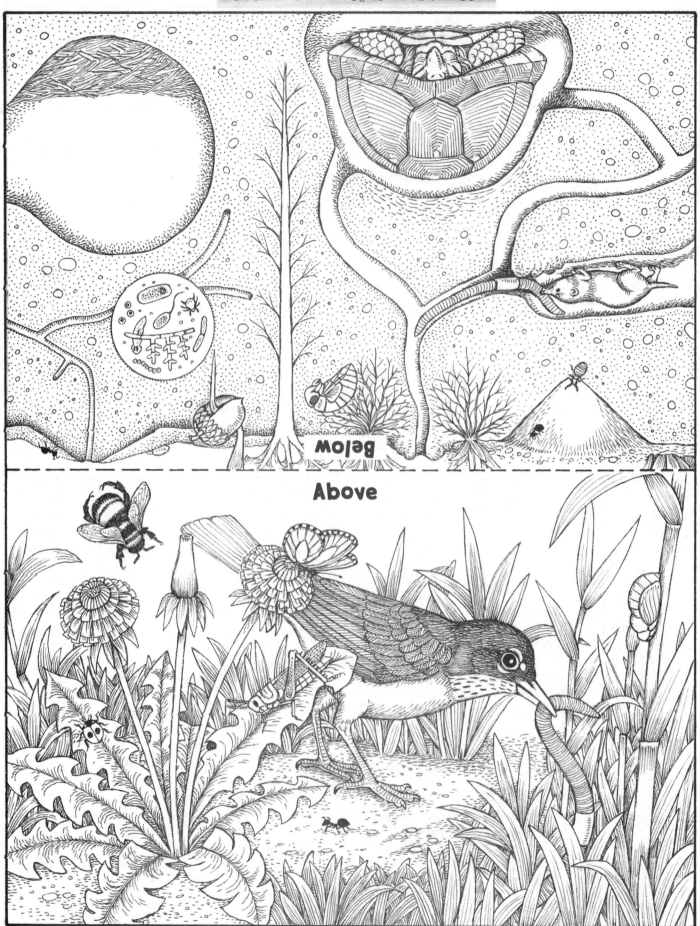

Below

Above

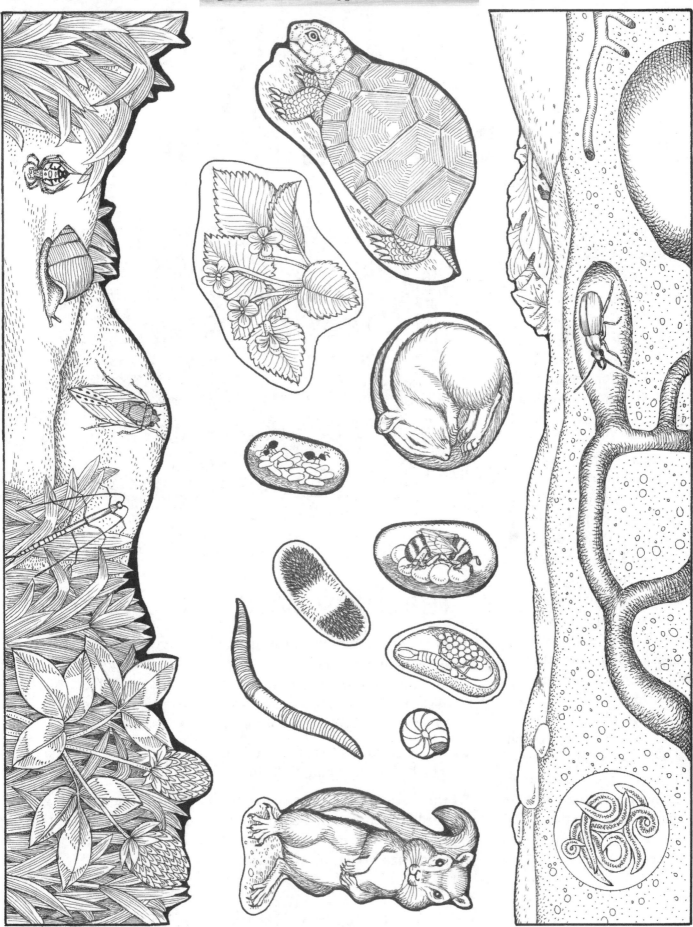

PARK
Day and Night

SCIENCE BACKGROUND

The Earth spins on its axis in a 24-hour cycle. During that cycle, the side of Earth facing the sun experiences daylight, while the opposite side experiences darkness or night.

Many animals roam about during the day. These animals take advantage of the sun's light to find food, water, and shelter. Some animals, however, sleep during the day and come out at night. To hunt for food and find their way in the dark, night animals depend on sharpened senses of sight, smell, and hearing. Bats, for example, send out very high-pitched sounds that bounce off objects and echo back to the bats' ears. The echoes tell bats where to fly without bumping into objects, and help them locate moths and other tasty insects.

Teaching with the Diorama

1. Engage students in a discussion about how your city or town appears during the daytime and at night. *(During the day, the sun is up and the sky is bright; streetlights are off. At night, the sun sets and the sky darkens; the moon and stars come out; electric lights illuminate streets, houses, and cars.)*

2. Invite students to assemble their Day and Night dioramas, which show day and night in a park. (See page 4.)

3. Have students turn to the Day side of the diorama. Using the border of the worksheet, have students identify each of the animals in the day scene. Ask, "How many animals do you recognize? What do you think each animal is doing?"

4. Turn to the Night side of the diorama. Have students identify each animal. Ask, "What do you think these nighttime animals do during the day?" *(Sleep, rest, or hide)* "What do daytime animals do at night?" *(Sleep, rest, or hide)*

5. Challenge students to use their dioramas to answer the questions on page 12.

Book Links

The Giant Book of Creatures of the Night
by Jim Pipe
(Copper Beech Books, 1998)

The Night Book: Exploring Nature After Dark With Activities, Experiments and Information
by Pamela Hickman
(Kids Can Press, 1999)

Night Creatures
by Gallinard Jeunesse
(Scholastic, 1998)

Answers

1. Day
2. Night
3. During the day, the morning glory's petals are open. At night, it closes up.
4. On a tree branch
5. Lightning bug
6. Night
7. Three
8. Night
9. Answers may vary. Possible answers could include: There are less predators and it's easier to hide.
10. Answers will vary.

Explore More!

What causes day and night?

Explain to students that the Earth rotates, or spins, on its axis in a 24-hour cycle, causing day to alternate with night. Help students locate your hometown on a globe. Give one student volunteer the globe (tilted on its axis), and another volunteer a flashlight to represent the sun. As the first student slowly turns the globe counterclockwise from the top, have the other student aim the flashlight on the Earth. (You may want to darken the room.) Invite students to call out "day" or "night" as your hometown spins past the sun's light. Locate another country, such as China, on the other side of the globe so students can see that while the sun shines on one side of the world, the other side experiences night.

Day and Night

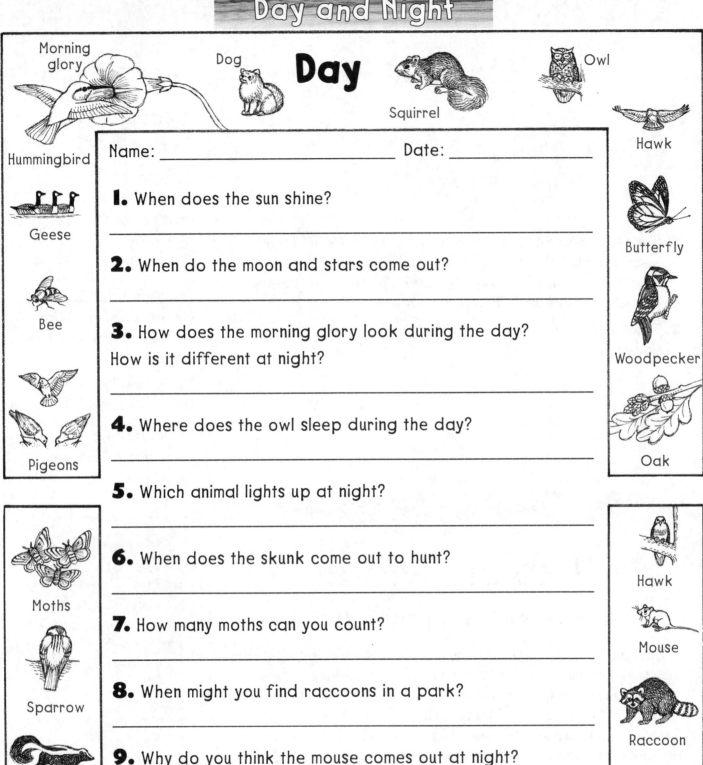

Day

Morning glory **Dog** **Squirrel** **Owl**

Hummingbird

Geese

Bee

Pigeons

Hawk

Butterfly

Woodpecker

Oak

Name: _____ Date: _____

1. When does the sun shine?

_____

2. When do the moon and stars come out?

_____

3. How does the morning glory look during the day?
How is it different at night?

_____

4. Where does the owl sleep during the day?

_____

5. Which animal lights up at night?

_____

6. When does the skunk come out to hunt?

_____

7. How many moths can you count?

_____

8. When might you find raccoons in a park?

_____

9. Why do you think the mouse comes out at night?

_____

10. Which do you like better—day or night? On the back
of this page, write why you prefer day or night.

Moths

Sparrow

Skunk

Nightjar

Hawk

Mouse

Raccoon

Pigeons

Bat **Morning glory**

Night

 **Lightning bugs**

 Owl

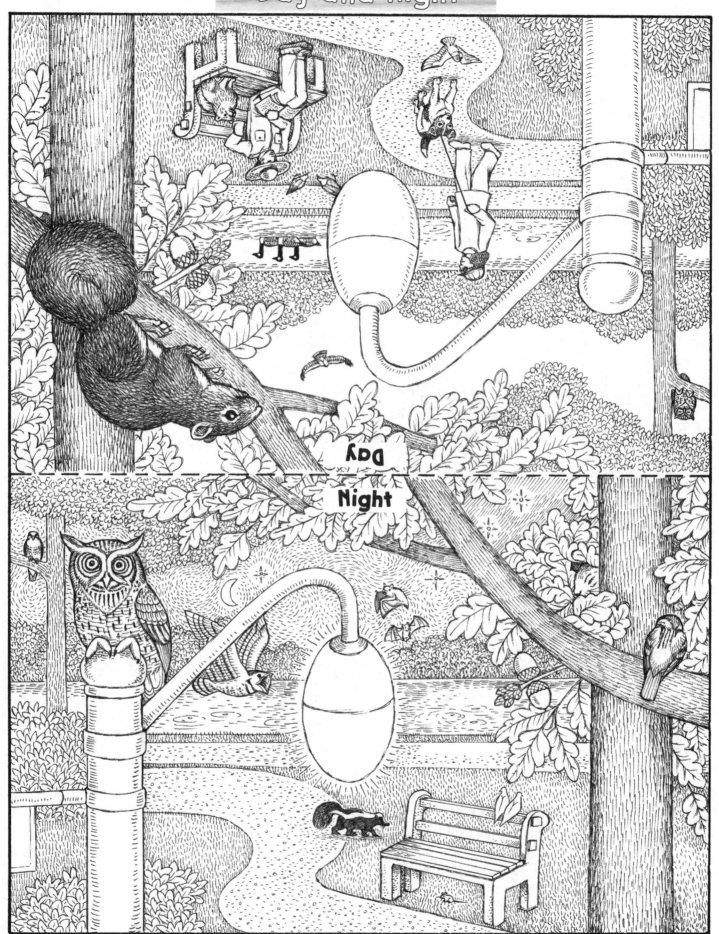

Pond
Summer and Winter

Teaching with the Diorama

1. Invite students to draw pictures of your town or city in winter and summer. (If you live in a warm climate, have students envision a town or city up north.) Compare the pictures and discuss what the weather is like, what people are wearing, what animals are doing, and what plants look like.

2. Have students assemble their Summer and Winter dioramas, which feature a pond. (See page 4.) Explain that a pond is a small body of water surrounded by land.

3. Ask students to turn to the Winter side of the diorama. Ask, "What do the pond animals do in the winter?" *(Some pond animals, such as turtles and frogs, sleep in the mud at the bottom of the pond. Fish move slowly in the frigid water under the ice.)* Explain that in places where winter is cold, a

SCIENCE BACKGROUND

The Earth spins on its own axis as it travels around the sun in a 365-day orbit. Earth's axis is tilted. This affects how much sunlight falls on different parts of our planet at different times of the year. For example, the Northern Hemisphere leans toward the sun in June, making the days long and hot—summer. In December, when the Earth is on the other side of the sun, the Southern Hemisphere leans toward the sun. The Northern Hemisphere experiences winter.

Book Links

In the Small, Small Pond
by Denise Fleming
(Henry Holt, 1998)

Around the Pond: Who's Been Here?
by Lindsay Barrett George
(Greenwillow Books, 1996)

Pond Year
by Kathryn Lasky
(Candlewick Press, 1997)

When Summer Comes
by Robert Maass
(Henry Holt, 1996)

Answers

1. There is snow and ice on the pond.
2. Summer
3. A thin layer of ice
4. Summer
5. Water lily, cattail
6. Answers will vary.
7. Asleep in the mud
8. Crow
9. The ice is thin and might break.
10. Answers will vary.

thin layer of ice may form over a pond's surface. This ice keeps the water underneath from freezing and protects the living things below.

4. Turn to the Summer side. Ask, "How does the pond change in the summer?" (*In summer, the pond is full of life. Baby animals born in spring are growing. Water lilies and other plants grow in the water and at the pond's edge.*) Point out the microscopic plankton inside the circle. Explain that plankton are tiny algae and animals that provide food for tadpoles, small fish, and other small water creatures. Have students research what each animal in the pond eats.

5. Challenge students to use their dioramas to answer the questions on page 17.

Explore More!

Why do we have seasons?

Put a desk lamp (the "sun") in the center of the floor. (Remove the lamp shade.) Mark four equally spaced positions around it about 3 feet away. Label these points March, June, September, and December. Place a globe at December, with the South Pole tilted toward the lamp. If necessary, stack books beneath the globe to align the top of the globe with the lamp's bulb. Slowly turn the globe counterclockwise from the top. Ask, "How much daylight does the South Pole get during day? How about the North Pole? How about places in between?" Repeat this activity for March, June, and September. (Be sure the Earth keeps its tilt as it "revolves around the sun.") Have students describe how daylight changes around the world during each season.

Summer

Minnows

Turtle

Yellow perch

Catfish

Crayfish

Clam

Newt

Frog eggs

Giant water bug

Whirligig beetle

Water lily

Dragonfly

Frog and tadpole

Plankton

Cattail

Name: _____ Date: _____

1. How can you tell it's winter at the pond?

_____

2. In which season are more animals in the pond?

_____

3. What covers the pond in winter?

_____

4. When are there frog eggs in the pond?

_____

5. Name a plant that grows in the summer pond.

_____

6. Name an animal that is in the summer pond but not the winter pond.

_____

7. Where is the frog in the winter pond?

_____

8. Which animal left footprints in the snow?

_____

9. Why should you never walk or skate on pond ice?

_____

10. On the back of this page, describe how the winter pond is different from the summer pond.

Crow

Hibernating frog

Snail

Bluegill

Hibernating newt

Clam in mud

Water beetle

Waterlily tuber

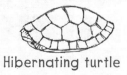

Hibernating turtle

Winter

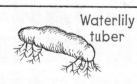

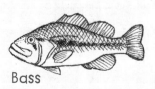

Bass

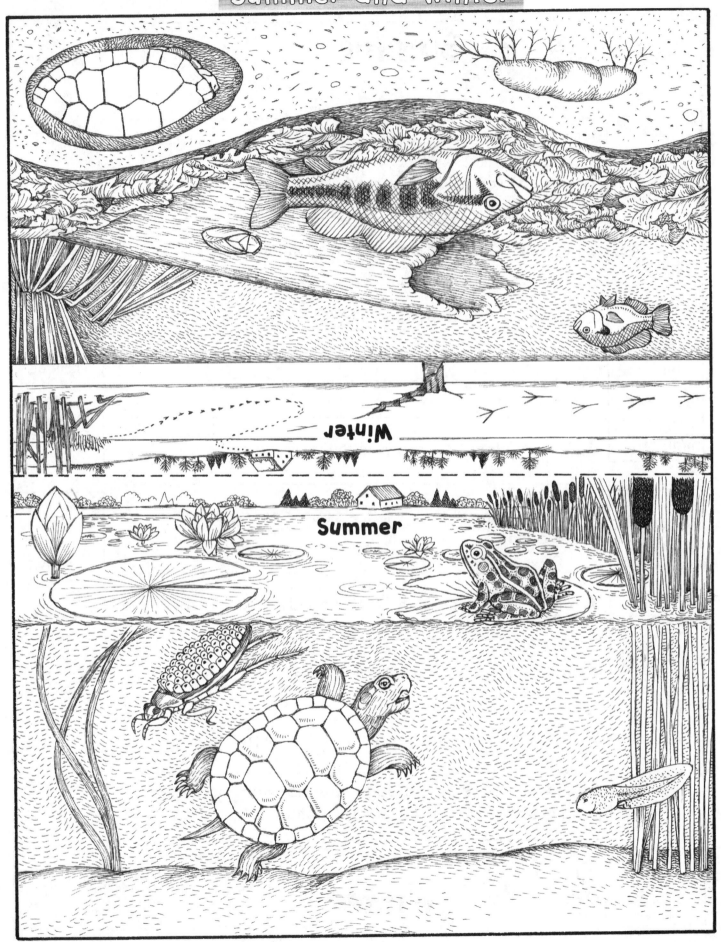

Winter

Summer

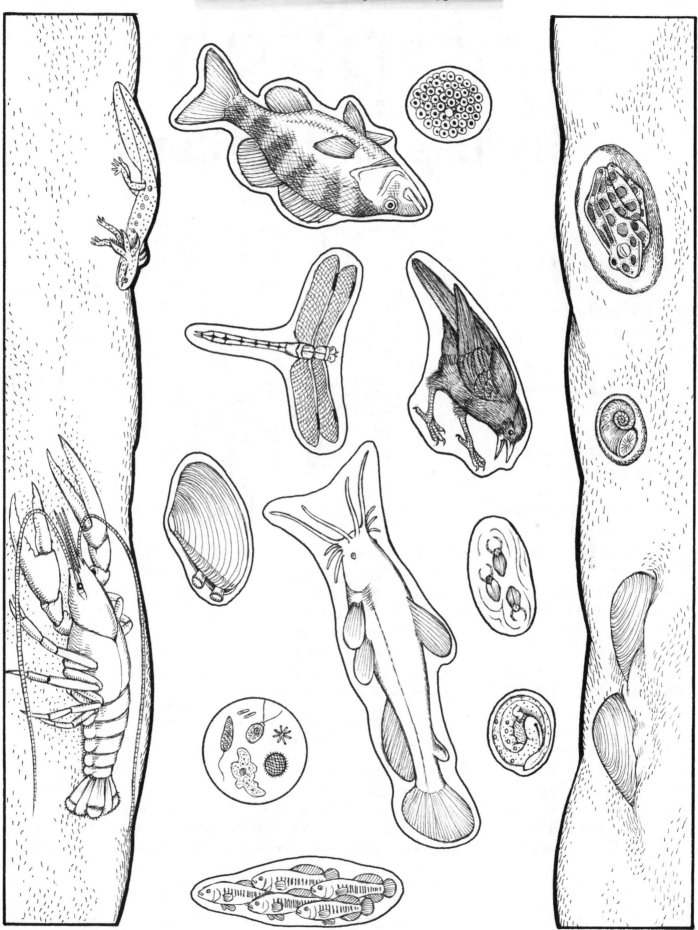

FOREST
Spring and Autumn

Spring and autumn bring about changes that are perhaps most noticeable in a deciduous forest. In autumn, the leaves of deciduous trees change colors. ***Chlorophyll,*** the pigment (coloring material) that gives leaves their green color, helps plants use the sun's energy to make food. In autumn, as days grow shorter, chlorophyll production slows down and stops. The leaves produce other pigments that make yellow, orange, red, or gold colors. Then the leaves fall. The point where each leaf breaks from its branch seals shut so water cannot escape from the plant. Plants without leaves need less water to survive the winter months. In spring, as days grow longer, chlorophyll production increases and new green leaves appear.

Teaching with the Diorama

1. Invite students to describe the changes that take place in autumn. *(The weather gets colder and leaves turn color and fall to the ground.)* If you do not live in a place where such changes occur, bring in pictures of trees with their fall colors. Ask students, "How do autumn days differ from spring days?" *(Days get cooler as autumn progresses and the sun sets earlier. Spring days get warmer with more and more daylight as summer approaches.)*

2. Invite students to assemble their Spring and Autumn dioramas, which feature a deciduous forest. (See page 4.)

3. Have students turn to the Spring side of the diorama. Point out the budding leaves and flowers on and around the tree. Explain that spring rains are vital for plant growth. Ask students, "What else begins to grow in the spring?" *(Many animals' babies are born in spring and begin to grow. Insects*

hatch out of their eggs and butterflies emerge from their chrysalises.) As eggs hatch and young animals grow and develop the woods become more and more active.

4. Turn to the Autumn side. Explain that as the weather grows colder, the roots, trunks, and branches of deciduous plants store food made by their leaves. Ask students, "How do animals prepare for winter?" *(Some birds and butterflies migrate to warmer places. Squirrels hide nuts, and mice and chipmunks store seeds in their underground burrows. Many insects lay eggs and then die, while some caterpillars spin cocoons or chrysalises.)* As winter approaches, the autumn woods become less and less active.

5. Challenge students to use their dioramas to answer the questions on page 22.

Explore More!

How do seeds get around?

   In the fall, many plants scatter their seeds so new plants can sprout and grow in the spring. How do seeds get around? Have students examine various seeds (sunflower, burdock, maple, etc.) with a hand lens and think about what helps these seeds travel. Divide the class into small groups and distribute 10 kernels of uncooked popcorn (the "seeds") to each group. Challenge students to invent ways to help their seeds travel at least one foot away from their starting point. Provide cotton balls, tissue paper, string, paper, Velcro, glue, and other materials for students to use. Test their seeds by holding each one about 4 inches in front of a gently blowing fan. Which design helped the seeds travel the farthest?

Book Links

Autumn Leaves
by Ken Robbins
(Scholastic, 1998)

Red Leaf, Yellow Leaf
by Lois Ehlert
(Harcourt Brace, 1991)

Spring Across America
by Seymour Simon
(Hyperion, 1996)

When Spring Comes
by Robert Maass
(Henry Holt, 1996)

Answers
1. Autumn
2. Oak
3. Spring beauty, dogwood, columbine, oak flower
4. Mantis, stag beetle, monarch butterfly
5. In a nest
6. Woodpecker
7. Acorn
8. Spring
9. In its cocoon
10. Answers will vary.

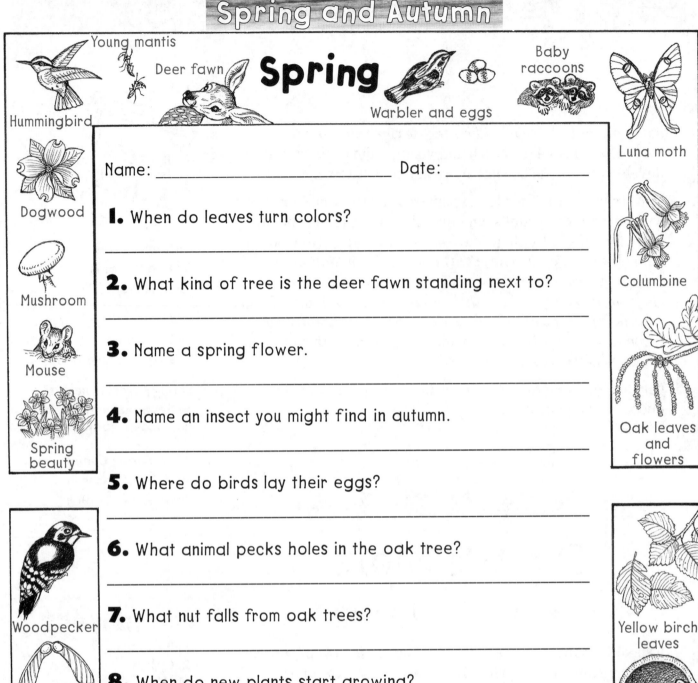

Spring

Hummingbird
Young mantis
Deer fawn
Warbler and eggs
Baby raccoons
Luna moth
Dogwood
Columbine
Mushroom
Mouse
Spring beauty
Oak leaves and flowers

Name: _____ Date: _____

1. When do leaves turn colors?

_____

2. What kind of tree is the deer fawn standing next to?

_____

3. Name a spring flower.

_____

4. Name an insect you might find in autumn.

_____

5. Where do birds lay their eggs?

_____

6. What animal pecks holes in the oak tree?

_____

7. What nut falls from oak trees?

_____

8. When do new plants start growing?

_____

9. Where does the luna moth caterpillar spend the winter?

_____

10. Which season do you like better—spring or autumn? On the back of this page explain why.

Woodpecker
Elm seed
Oak buds and acorn

Yellow birch leaves
Raccoon in nest
Monarch butterfly

Mantis and egg case
Luna moth caterpillar and cocoon
Larva
Stag beetle
Blueberries

Autumn

eggs

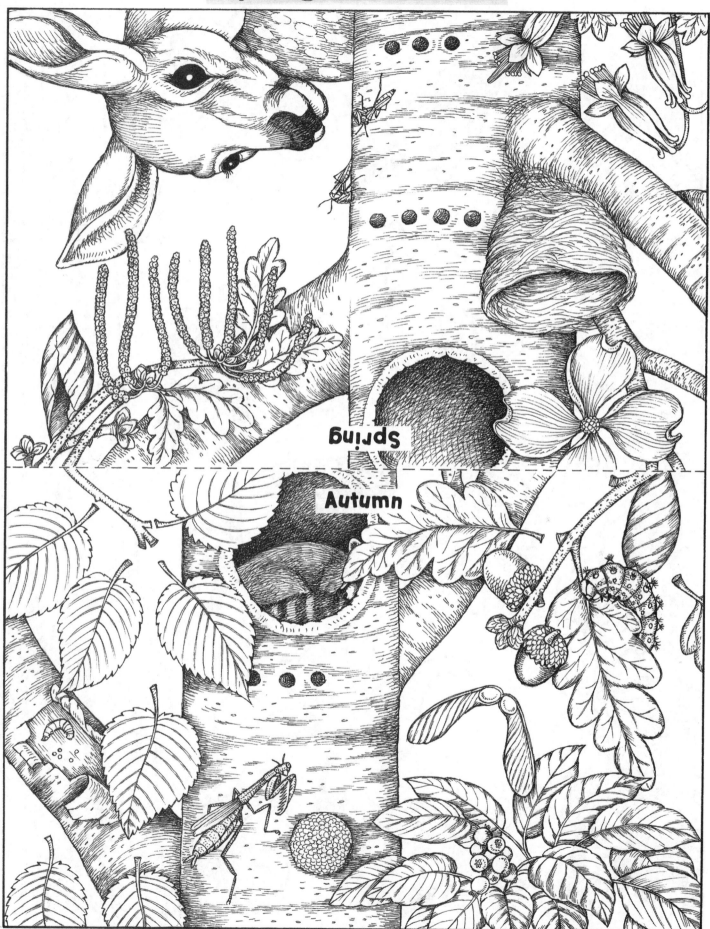

Spring

Autumn

Spring and Autumn

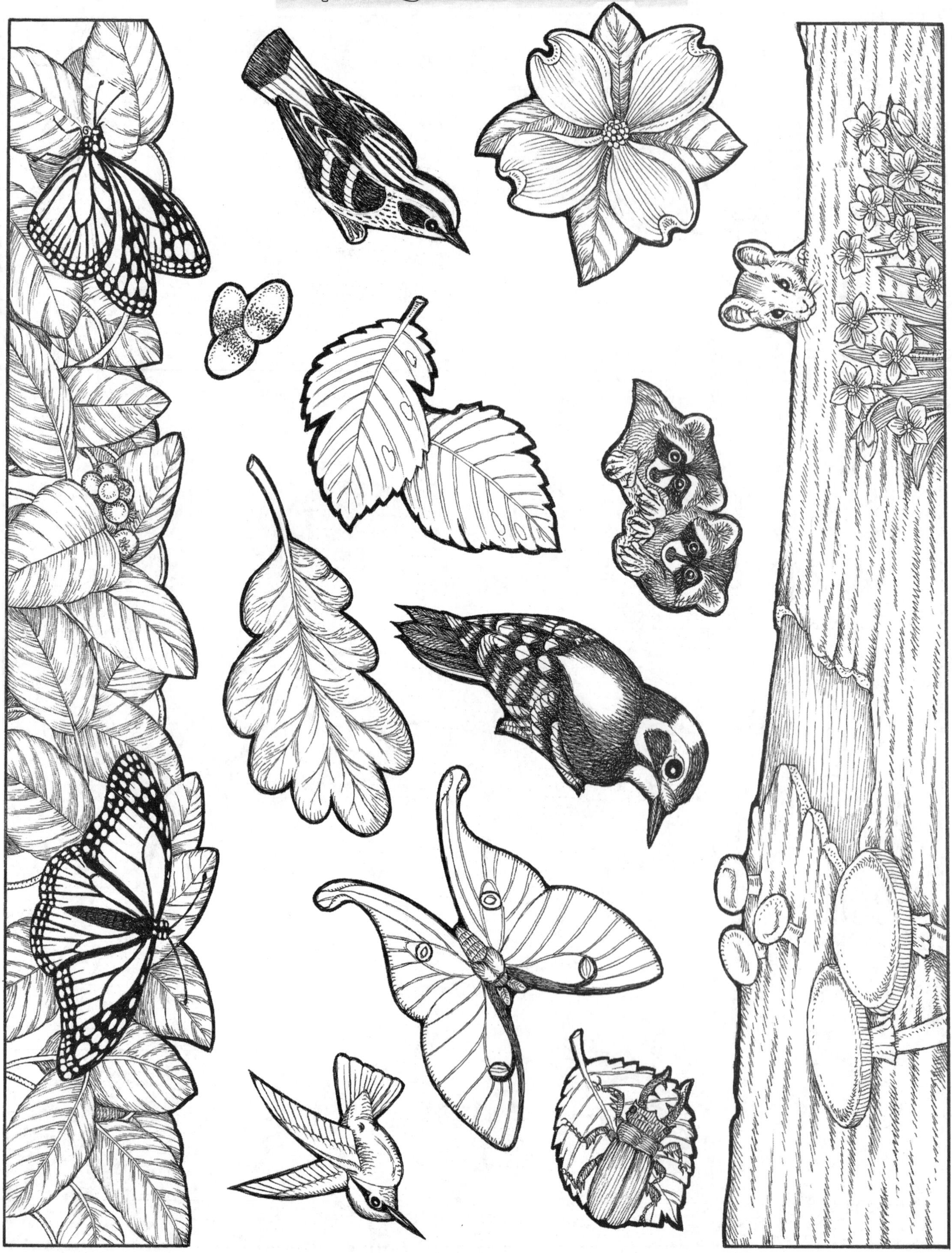

Cave
Front and Back

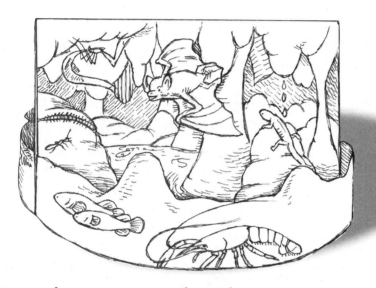

Teaching with the Diorama

1. Ask students, "What do you think of when you hear the word 'cave'?" List their responses on the board. Find out if any students have explored a cave or seen one in a movie or magazine. Have them describe what they remember. Bring in pictures of Carlsbad Caverns in New Mexico or other well-known caves to show to your class.

2. Invite students to assemble their Front and Back dioramas, which feature a cave. (See page 4.) On the Front side of the diorama, help students cut out the cave opening (surrounded by the solid black line). Have them cut out the group of flying bats with the flap. Tape the flap to the back of the diorama so that the bats show through the cave opening.

3. Have students turn to the Front part of the cave. Explain that this part of a cave, called the *twilight zone*, is dimly lit by

Most caves form in limestone rock. Water seeps into the rock and dissolves the limestone before carrying it away. Over long periods of time, this process results in the formation of underground chambers. Large limestone caves are called *caverns*. Other types of caves include *ice caves* that form in glaciers and icebergs, *sea caves* formed by wave action in cliff rocks, *lava caves* that form in lava as it hardens into rock, and caves formed by the eroding action of rivers.

Book Links

Amazing Bats
by Frank Greenaway
(Alfred A. Knopf, 1991)

One Small Square: Cave
by Donald M. Silver
(McGraw-Hill, 1997)

daylight that comes in through the opening. Ask, "What plants and animals live in this part of the cave?" *(Ferns, moss, mushrooms, pack rats, frogs, salamanders, barn owls, swallows)* Some animals, such as deer and skunks, may also wander in and out. A bear may give birth to her cubs in this part of a cave, and garter snakes, frogs, and toads may sleep here during winter.

4. Turn to the Back part of the cave. This part is a zone of total darkness—no sunlight reaches the back of the cave so no plants can grow there. Ask, "How do you think animals that live in here find their way around the dark?" *(Many animals, like bats, rely on their hearing and other senses.)* Explain that some animals that live in the back of the cave are blind or may even have no eyes. Instead they use highly developed senses of smell and touch to detect food and enemies in the dark.

5. Challenge students to use their dioramas to answer the questions on page 27.

Explore More!
How do stalactites form?

Stalactites, "icicles" that hang from cave roofs, form when groundwater seeping down into the cave picks up minerals from the limestone rock and drips from the cave roof. To grow a stalactite, fill two plastic cups 1/3 full with Epsom salts. Very carefully, fill the cups with hot water and stir until the Epsom salts dissolve. Fold a 30-inch-long piece of cotton string or wool yarn in half. Twist the two halves together, then dip the string into one cup to wet it thoroughly. Tie each end of the string to a paper clip and put it into the cups, as shown.

Place a plastic plate between the cups. The bottom of the string should be about an inch above the plate. After a few days, you'll see a stalactite form.

Answers
1. Answers will vary.
2. Back
3. Blind cave beetle, blind centipede, blind Ozark cave salamander, blind cave fish
4. They hang upside down.
5. Moss, mushrooms, ferns
6. To hunt for food outside the cave
7. Blind cave fish
8. Blind centipede
9. Stalactites and stalagmites
10. Answers will vary.

Stalactite

Solitary bat

Back

Cave crayfish

Bat

Stalagmite

Cave cricket

Blind cave beetle

Bats

Blind ozark cave salamander

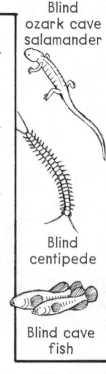

Blind centipede

Blind cave fish

Name: _____ Date: _____

1. Name two animals in the front of the cave.

_____

2. Which part of the cave is always dark?

_____

3. Name four cave animals that cannot see.

_____

4. How do bats cling to the inside of a cave?

_____

5. Name something that grows in the front of the cave.

6. Why do bats leave the cave at night?

_____

7. What swims in the pool at the back of the cave?

_____

8. Which animal living in the cave has the most legs?

_____

9. What are rock "icicles" inside a cave called?

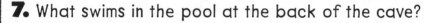

10. Long ago, people used to live in caves. On the back of this page, write what it might have been like to live in a cave.

Barn owl and chicks

Fern

Snail

Mushrooms

Barn swallows and nests

Frog

Moss

Pack rat

Returning bats

Front

Returning bat

Salamander

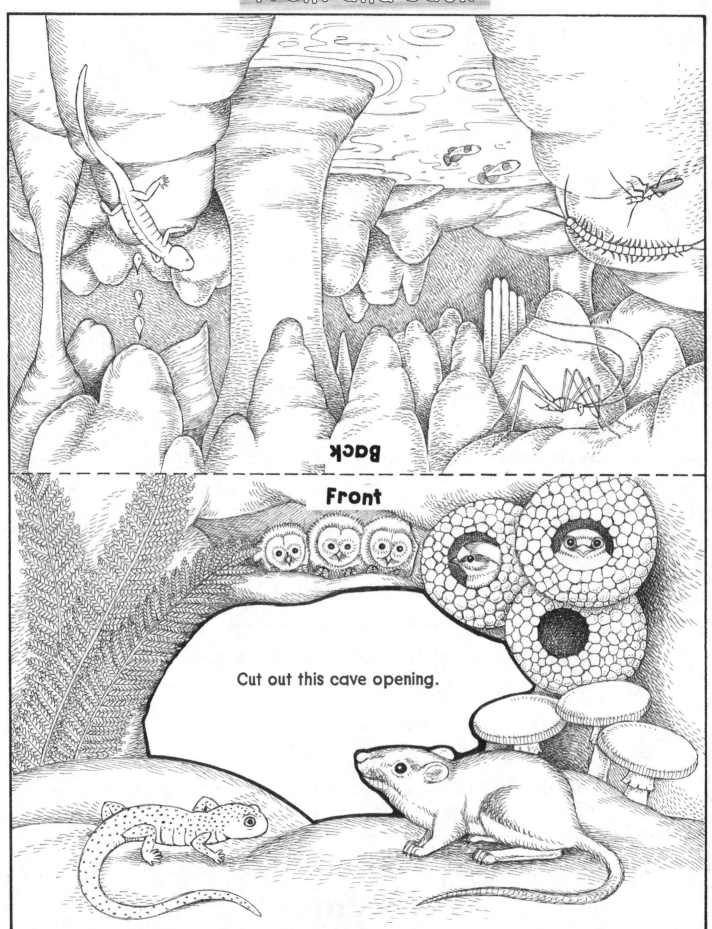

Back

Front

Cut out this cave opening.

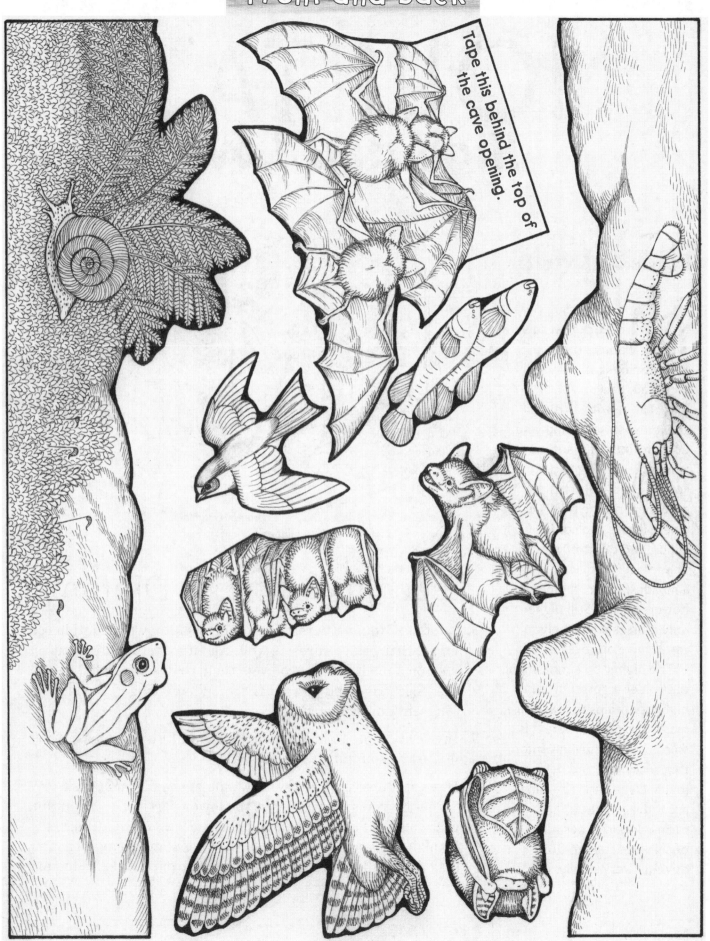

Tape this behind the top of the cave opening.

MOUNTAIN
High and Low

SCIENCE BACKGROUND

Mountains are peaks of rock that tower above the surrounding land. Every mountain has life zones that change with altitude above the surrounding land. Certain kinds of plants and animals survive in each zone. For example, tall trees don't grow beyond the *tree line*, where it gets too cold, windy, and dry for trees. The forest is replaced by a meadow where alpine flowers bloom. Still higher, only mosses and lichens can survive on rocks.

The higher up a mountain, the colder it gets. On very high mountains the *snow line* marks the point where it is so cold and windy in winter that snow falls and never melts. Over time, the snow accumulates, packs, and forms *glaciers*. These rivers of thick ice start to flow downhill very slowly.

Teaching with the Diorama

1. Point out Mount Everest and other well-known mountains on a map. Bring in pictures as well. Ask if any students have been on a mountain. Encourage them to describe what it was like. Ask, "How did you get there? What changed the higher you went on the mountain?"

2. Invite students to make their High and Low dioramas, which feature a mountain. (See page 4.)

3. Have students turn to the Low side of the diorama. Ask, "What do you see growing at the lower part of the mountain that you can't see at the high part?" *(Plants, including trees)* Explain that conifers, or trees with needlelike leaves that stay green all winter, grow in the lower part. Ask, "Why do

you think trees don't grow at the high part of the mountain?" *(It is too cold and windy for trees to survive.)*

4. Turn to the High side and point out the animals that live there. Explain that few animals live so high, and those that do tend to migrate downhill in winter to find food and shelter. Others hibernate through winter or burrow under the snow. Mountain sheep and goats grow thick fur to help them withstand the cold. They also have special rock-gripping hooves for jumping from rock to rock without slipping and falling.

5. Challenge students to use their dioramas to answer the questions on page 32.

Book Links

How Mountains Are Made
by Kathleen Weidner Zoehfeld
(Harper Trophy, 1995)

Mountains
by Seymour Simon
(Econo-Clad, 1999)

Mountains and Valleys
by Steve Parker
(Thunder Bay Press, 1996)

Explore More!

How well can students jump?

Challenge students to test their jumping abilities against mountain animals. The chamois, a small goat-like antelope, can leap 23 feet in a single bound from a standing start. How far away can your students jump from a starting point and land with both feet on the ground? The mountain lion can spring 13 feet straight up without a starting run. How high can your students jump straight up? (To measure, tape a yardstick on a wall and have students stand next to it and jump. Measure the highest point that their feet reach off the ground.)

Answers
1. High
2. Low
3. High
4. Brown bear
5. Golden eagle
6. Elk, brown bear, beaver, porcupine, squirrel, wolf, lynx, moose, pine marten
7. Mountain goat, dall sheep, elk, moose
8. Alpine flowers
9. High
10. Answers will vary.

High and Low

High

Glacier

Golden eagle

Clouds

Mountain goat and kid

Lichens

Grizzly bear and cubs

Ptarmigan

Dall sheep

Pica

Marmot

Alpine flower

Name: _____   Date: _____

1. Does the mountain goat live in the high or low part of the mountain?

_____

2. In which part do the beavers live?

_____

3. In which part do ptarmigans live?

_____

4. What kind of bear lives in the low part of the mountain?

_____

5. Name a bird that flies high up the mountain.

_____

6. Name three furry animals that live low on the mountain.

_____

7. Name an animal with horns or antlers.

_____

8. Name a plant that grows up high.

_____

9. Where do glacier start to form?

_____

10. On the back of this page, write a story about climbing a mountain. Use the names of 10 plants or animals you see in your diorama.

Squirrel

Beavers

Lynx

Pine marten

Wolf

Conifer and cone

Brown bear

Nutcracker

Moose

Aspen   Mountain bluebird

Low

Owl

Swan

Porcupine

Elk

Low

High

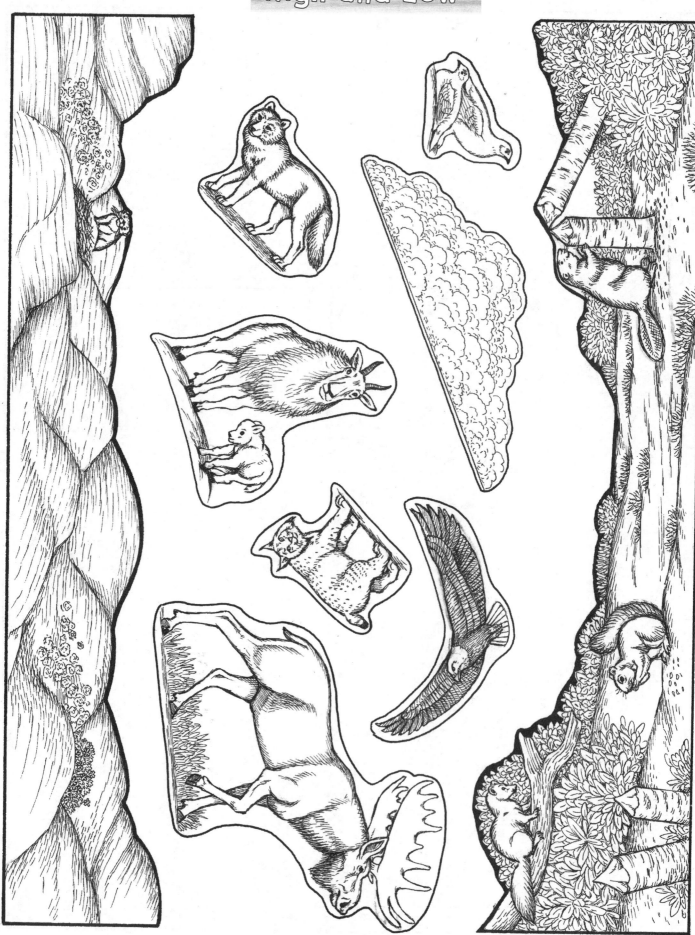

AFRICAN SAVANNA
Big and Little

Teaching with the Diorama

1. Encourage students to imagine what it would be like to be ants. Ask, "What might look big to an ant but little to a child?" *(A blade of grass or a pebble, for example)* Now have students imagine that they are elephants. Ask, "What objects might be little to an elephant but big to a child?" *(A car, for example)*

2. Invite students to assemble their Big and Little dioramas, which feature animals that live on the African savanna. (See page 4.)

3. Have students turn to the Big side of the diorama, which shows some of the biggest animals on the savanna. Ask students, "Why do you think the baby elephant is shown on the

SCIENCE BACKGROUND

The African savanna is mostly flat, open grassland where few trees and shrubs grow. The savanna stretches across parts of Central Africa south of the Sahara Desert.

The largest animal in the savanna is the African elephant, which can grow up to 24.5 feet long and weigh up to 14,000 pounds. The tallest creature is the giraffe, which stands up to 19.5 feet tall, with legs about 6 feet long. The smallest animal in this diorama is the termite, which is drawn actual size inside the circle (3/16 of an inch). Millions of these tiny termites can build a mound (or nest) up to 15 feet high.

Book Links

One Small Square: African Savanna
by Donald M. Silver
(McGraw-Hill, 1997)

Here Is the African Savanna
by Madeleine Dunphy
(Hyperion, 1999)

Hey, Little Ant
by Phillip and Hannah
Hoose
(Tricycle Press, 1998)

Peoples of the Savanna
by Robert Low
(Rosen Publishing, 1996)

Answers
1. Answers will vary.
2. Answers will vary.
3. Giraffe
4. In a termite mound
5. Rhinoceros, dik-dik,
Thompson's gazelle
6. Three
7. In the grass
8. Lion, crocodile
9. It is swimming, cooling
off, resting, etc.
10. Answers will vary.

Big side?" (*Even as a baby, the elephant is bigger than many other animals.*) Ask, "What is one advantage of being big?" (*Big animals are often stronger and can better protect themselves from other predators.*)

4. Have students turn to the Little side. Explain that the dik-dik on the rocks stands only 14 inches tall, while the Thompson's gazelle grows about 3.5 feet long. The civet grows less than 3 feet long. Ask, "What is one advantage of being little?" (*Little animals can hide easily from predators and find shelter in tiny crevices.*)

5. Challenge students to use their dioramas to answer the questions on page 37.

Explore More!

How do some animals in the savannah measure up?

Encourage students to research the sizes of other animals in the savanna. Then have them create a life-size bar graph on a wall, showing the sizes of the different animals. Include the average height of your students for comparison.

Big and Little

Big

Hippopotamus

Crocodile

Elephant

Baby elephant

Rhinoceros

Lion

Giraffe

Name: _____   Date: _____

1. Name a big African animal.

_____

2. Name a little African animal.

_____

3. Which African animal is tallest?

_____

4. Where do termites live?

_____

5. Name an animal with a horn on its head.

_____

6. How many hyraxes do you see?

_____

7. Where is the pygmy mouse?

_____

8. Name a big African animal that is a hunter.

_____

9. What is the hippopotamus doing?

_____

10. Choose a big or little animal as a pet. On the back of this page, write a story about your pet and what makes it special.

Dik-dik

Elephant shrew

Mole rats

Thompson's gazelle

Termite

Rock hyraxes

Dung beetle

Dwarf mongoose

Pygmy mouse

 Civet cat

Little

 Termite frog

 Waxbill

Instant Habitat **37** Dioramas

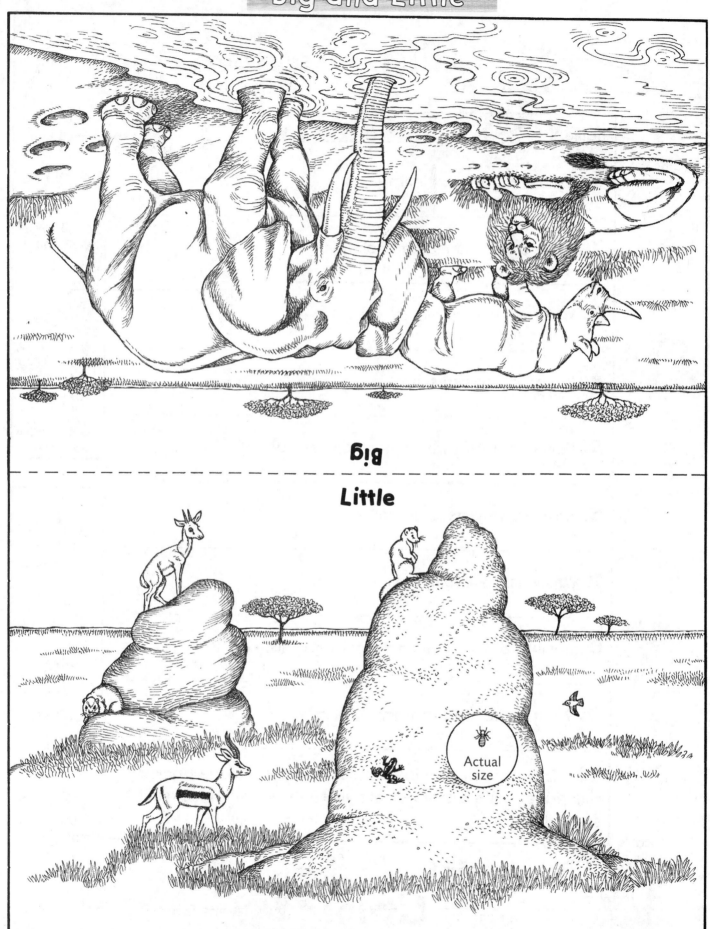

Big

Little

Actual size

Big and Little

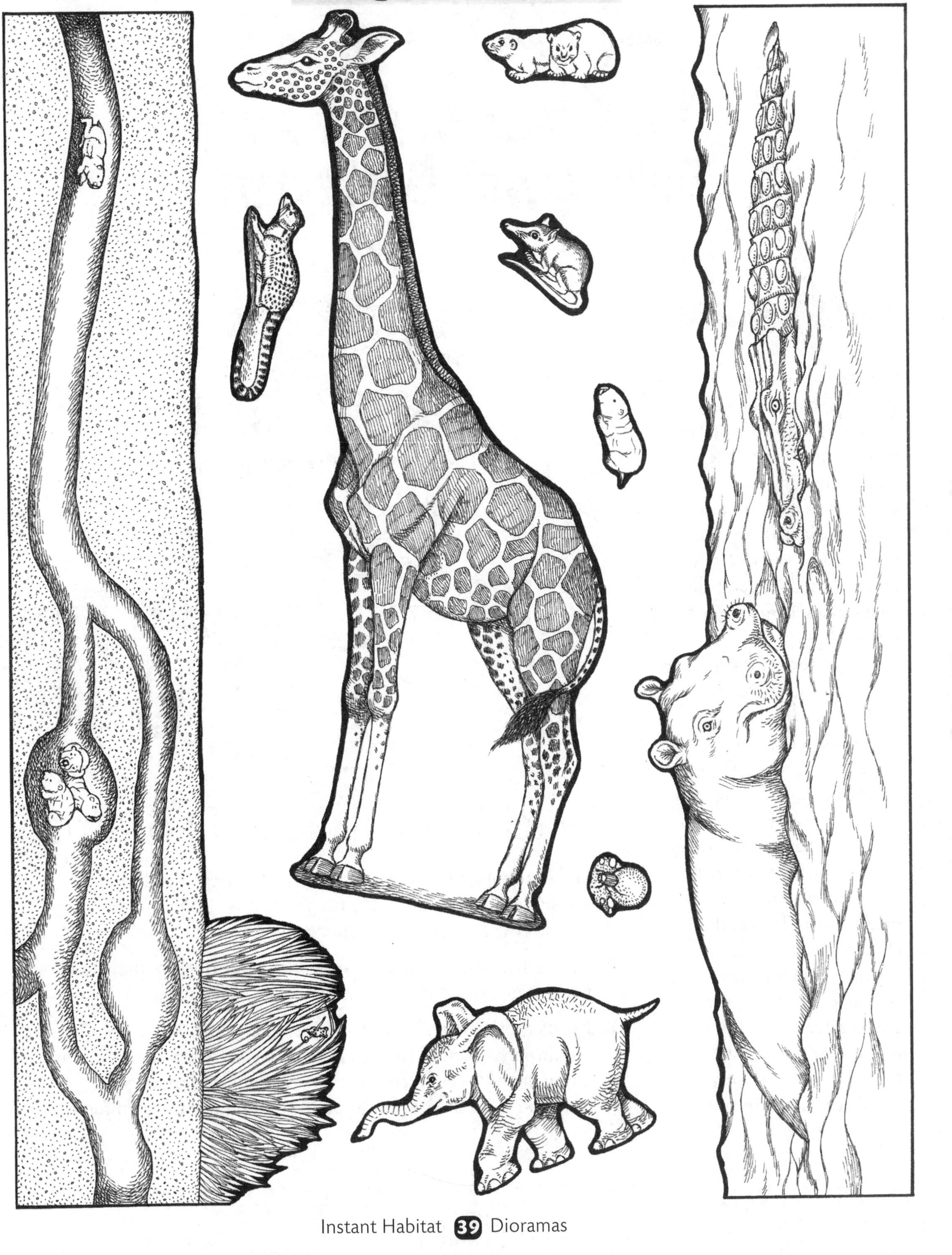

OCEAN
Top and Bottom

Oceans cover more than 70 percent of Earth. The top layer extends down to 500 feet and is lit by sunlight. Most sea animals live near the top of the ocean because there is so much food. *Plankton* provide food for small fish and huge blue whales. Large fish prey on small fish.

The bottom of the ocean is dark and near freezing. Few animals can withstand the tremendous pressure of the water above. Some deep-sea fish make their own light to attract prey and find mates. Chimney-shaped rocks called *black smokers* spew super-hot water filled with minerals and hydrogen-sulfide gas that cloud the water. Bacteria around these smokers feed on the minerals. Small deep-sea animals depend on the bacteria for food. Giant tube worms (some 8 to 10 feet long) also dwell near hot-water vents.

Teaching with the Diorama

1. Ask students, "Is our Earth covered mostly by land or water?" *(Water)* Bring in a map or globe. Point out that oceans cover more than 70 percent of Earth.

2. Invite students to assemble the Top and Bottom dioramas, which feature the mid-Atlantic ocean. (See page 4.)

3. Focus on the Top side of the diorama. Point out that plankton (shown in the circle) serves as food to many ocean animals and lives in the top layer, along with most sea animals. Like plants, some plankton make their own food

using energy from the sun. Ask students, "What do you think eats plankton?" *(Small fish and giant whales)* "What eats small fish?" *(Bigger fish)* Explain that animals and plants living in a habitat are linked together through the food they eat—this link is called a *food chain*.

4. Have students turn to the Bottom side of the diorama. Explain that the bottom of the mid-Atlantic ocean is about two miles deep. Unlike at the top layer of the ocean, very few animals live down here. Ask, "Why do you think that is?" *(The sun's light doesn't reach down there and so there's less food. Also, the weight of the water above is too much that few animals can survive the pressure.)*

5. Challenge students to use their dioramas to answer the questions on page 42.

Book Links

The Magic School Bus on the Ocean Floor
by Joanna Cole
(Scholastic, 1994)

Life in the Oceans
by Lucy Baker
(Scholastic, 1993)

Creeps from the Deep
by Leighton Taylor
(Chronicle Books, 1997)

Explore More!

Who eats what?

Invite students to create a mobile of sea creatures, illustrating the ocean food web. Have them draw or cut out pictures of various sea animals—from microscopic plankton to large whales—and glue the pictures onto oaktag. Have students tie the sea creatures to a wire hanger. The catch: Each predator must be placed next to its prey (for example, mackerel next to plankton and swordfish next to mackerel). Have students discuss who eats whom in the ocean.

Answers

1. Flashlight fish, lanternfish, anglerfish
2. Top
3. Top
4. Blue whale
5. Anglerfish, lanternfish
6. Giant tubeworms
7. Gull
8. Tripod fish, lanternfish
9. Sea turtle, nautilus
10. Answers will vary.

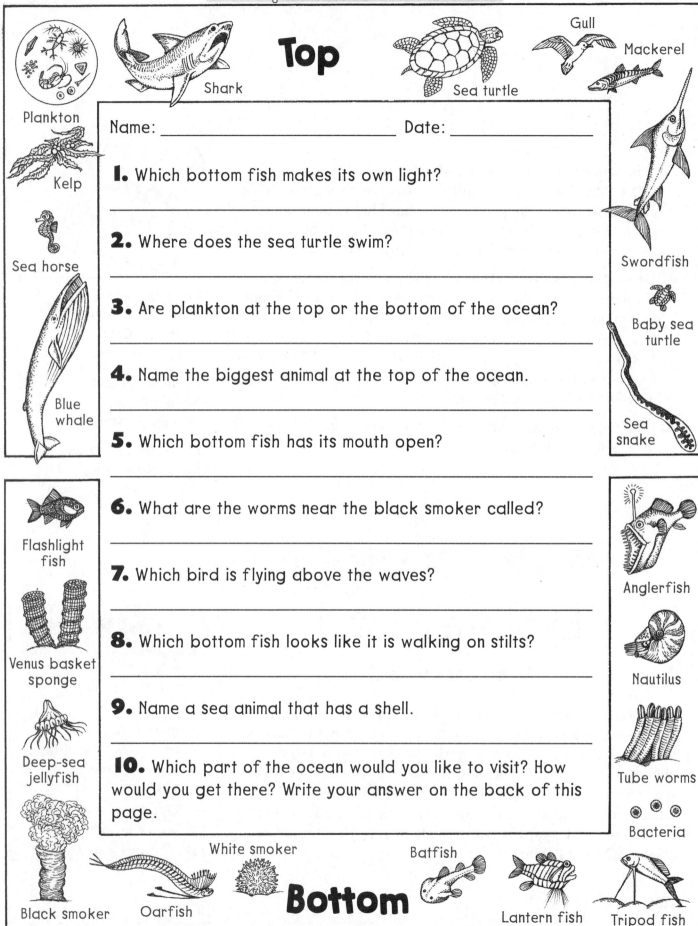

Top and Bottom

Top

Shark

Sea turtle

Gull

Mackerel

Plankton

Kelp

Sea horse

Blue whale

Swordfish

Baby sea turtle

Sea snake

Name: _____ Date: _____

1. Which bottom fish makes its own light?

_____

2. Where does the sea turtle swim?

_____

3. Are plankton at the top or the bottom of the ocean?

_____

4. Name the biggest animal at the top of the ocean.

_____

5. Which bottom fish has its mouth open?

6. What are the worms near the black smoker called?

_____

7. Which bird is flying above the waves?

_____

8. Which bottom fish looks like it is walking on stilts?

_____

9. Name a sea animal that has a shell.

_____

10. Which part of the ocean would you like to visit? How would you get there? Write your answer on the back of this page.

Flashlight fish

Venus basket sponge

Deep-sea jellyfish

Black smoker

Oarfish

White smoker

Bottom

Batfish

Lantern fish

Tripod fish

Anglerfish

Nautilus

Tube worms

Bacteria

Top

Bottom

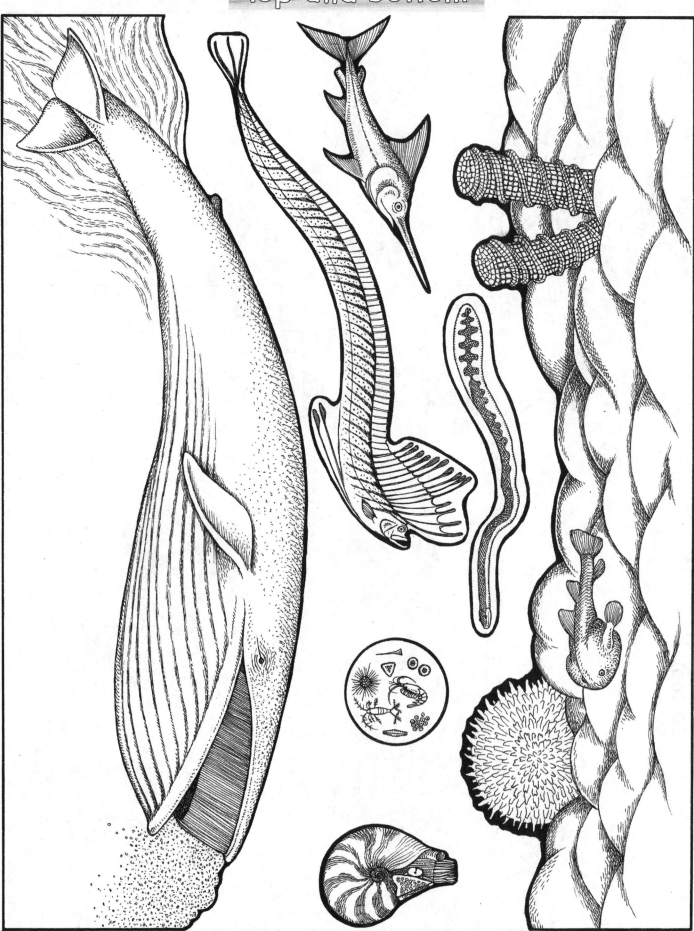

DESERT and TUNDRA
Hot and Cold

Teaching with the Diorama

1. Engage students in a discussion about hot and cold weather. Ask, "Does it get really hot where you live? What does it feel like outside on such a day? What do you do to keep cool?" Repeat the same questions about cold weather.

2. Have students assemble their Hot and Cold dioramas, which feature the Sonoran Desert in Arizona and the Arctic tundra in Northern Canada. (See page 4.)

3. If possible, locate the desert on a world map. Point out the Arctic tundra along the top of the Northwest Territories in Canada as well. Ask students, "What do you notice about where the desert and tundra lies in the map?" *(The desert is closer to the equator and the tundra is farther up north.)* Explain to students that places near the equator

Book Links

America's Deserts: Guide to Plants and Animals
by Marianne D. Wallace
(Fulcrum, 1996)

Arctic Tundra
by Michael H. Forman
(Children's Press, 1997)

get a lot of sun, and are therefore hot all year round. Regions farther up north get less sun and stay cold most of the time.

4. Turn to the Hot side. Ask, "How do you think animals survive in the hot desert?" *(They rest and hide from the sun during the day. Most animals get water from the foods they eat.)*

5. Have students turn to the Cold side. Ask, "How do you think these animals survive in such a cold environment?" *(They grow thick fur or feathers to stay warm. Some animals hide under the snow, which acts like a blanket.)*

6. Challenge students to use their dioramas to answer the questions on page 47.

Explore More!

What's the temperature around the world?

Create a giant wall thermometer with students to display the wide range of temperatures on Earth. Draw a large thermometer on butcher paper and mark off every 10 degrees from 150°F on top to –150°F at the bottom. Help students research record-breaking temperatures on Earth. For example, the lowest recorded temperature on Earth is at Vostok Station in Antarctica at –129.3°F. The highest recorded temperature is in Al Aziziyah, Libya, at 136.4°F. Have students mark the different temperatures on the thermometer and label the places. Encourage students to conduct research and add more entries to the thermometer. For example, the average temperature in the classroom, gym, cafeteria, or library; average human-body temperature; temperatures at which water boils and freezes, etc.

Answers
1. Answers will vary
2. Barrel cactus, ocotillo, saguaro
3. In a rock crack
4. It grows sharp spines.
5. Lizard
6. Jackrabbit
7. Under the snow
8. They grow thick fur.
9. In the Arctic tundra
10. Answers will vary.

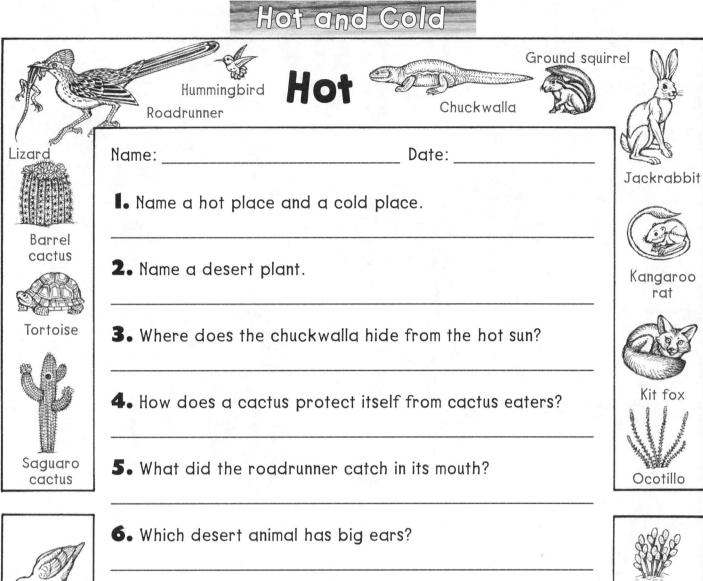

Hot

Roadrunner   Hummingbird   Chuckwalla   Ground squirrel

Lizard

Barrel cactus

Tortoise

Saguaro cactus

Jackrabbit

Kangaroo rat

Kit fox

Ocotillo

Name: _____   Date: _____

1. Name a hot place and a cold place.

_____

2. Name a desert plant.

_____

3. Where does the chuckwalla hide from the hot sun?

_____

4. How does a cactus protect itself from cactus eaters?

_____

5. What did the roadrunner catch in its mouth?

_____

6. Which desert animal has big ears?

_____

7. Where does the lemming hide from the bitter cold?

_____

8. How do the musk oxen stay warm?

_____

9. Where would you find an ermine?

_____

10. Say you're going on vacation to a very hot or very cold place. (Choose one.) On the back of this page, write the name of the place and list 10 things you will pack.

Ptarmigan

Arctic ground squirrel

Lemming

Dwarf willow

Arctic fox

Arctic hare

Raven   Ermine   ## Cold   Snowy owl   Musk ox

Hot

Cold

RAIN FOREST and Wet and Dry

Among the wettest parts of the world, tropical rain forests receive at least 80 inches of rain a year. In some forests, more than 200 inches of rain fall a year and a few get drenched with 400 inches. Because of so much wetness and warmth, a tropical rain forest supports lush plant growth. More kinds of plants and animals live in tropical rain forests than in any other habitat.

On the opposite end of the spectrum are deserts, which receive less than 10 inches of rain each year. The Sahara Desert, located in the northern third of Africa, is one of the driest deserts on Earth. About one-fifth of the desert is covered with sand. The rest is rocky or gravelly.

Teaching with the Diorama

1. Bring in a newspaper and, together with students, check how much precipitation fell over the last month. Ask students, "What happens when it rains a lot?" *(Floods may develop; soil washes away.)* "What happens if no rain falls for a long time?" *(There may be a water shortage; some plants whither and die.)* Challenge students to think of places where it rains a lot or where it hardly rains at all.

2. Invite students to make their Wet and Dry dioramas, which show an African rain forest and desert. (See page 4.)

3. Have students compare the rain forest to the desert. Ask, "What is different between the two habitats?" *(The rain forest has more plants and animals living in it. The desert is more bare and has fewer plants and animals.)* "Why do you

DESERT

think a lot of plants grow in the rain forest?" *(A lot of rain falls there, providing plants with lots of water, which they need to grow.)*

4. Turn to the Dry side of the diorama. Explain to students that desert animals and plants have adaptations that help them hold on to water even under the hot sun. Camels are a prime example of animals adapted to dry deserts. They can travel for days without water, surviving for long periods using fat (not water) stored in their humps. To replace fluids, some camels can drink about 18 gallons of water at a time. Ask, "How do you think desert plants stay moist?" *(Many desert plants have thick, waxy, outer walls that keep water inside. Some plants, like cacti, have sharp spines that protect them from thirsty animals.)*

5. Challenge students to use their dioramas to answer the questions on page 52.

Book Links

The Rain Forest
by Gallimard Jeunesse
(Scholastic, 1994)

Desert
by Miranda MacQuitty
(Dorling Kindersley, 2000)

Explore More!

How do plants keep water in?

To keep moisture in, many desert plants have a waxy coating on their stems and leaves. How effective is a waxy coating for keeping water in? Wet three paper towels and spread one towel on a cookie sheet. Take the second towel and roll it up. Take the third one, roll it up, and wrap it in wax paper. Tape the ends closed. Place both rolled-up towels on the cookie sheet next to the first towel. Put the cookie sheet in a warm, dry place and leave there for one day. Which paper towel kept water in best?

Answers
1. Hornbill, Congo peacock, gray parrot
2. In the rain forest
3. Adult okapi
4. Rain forest
5. Liana vine
6. Camel
7. Sand
8. Acacia
9. There are no clouds in the sky and the sun is shining.
10. Answers will vary.

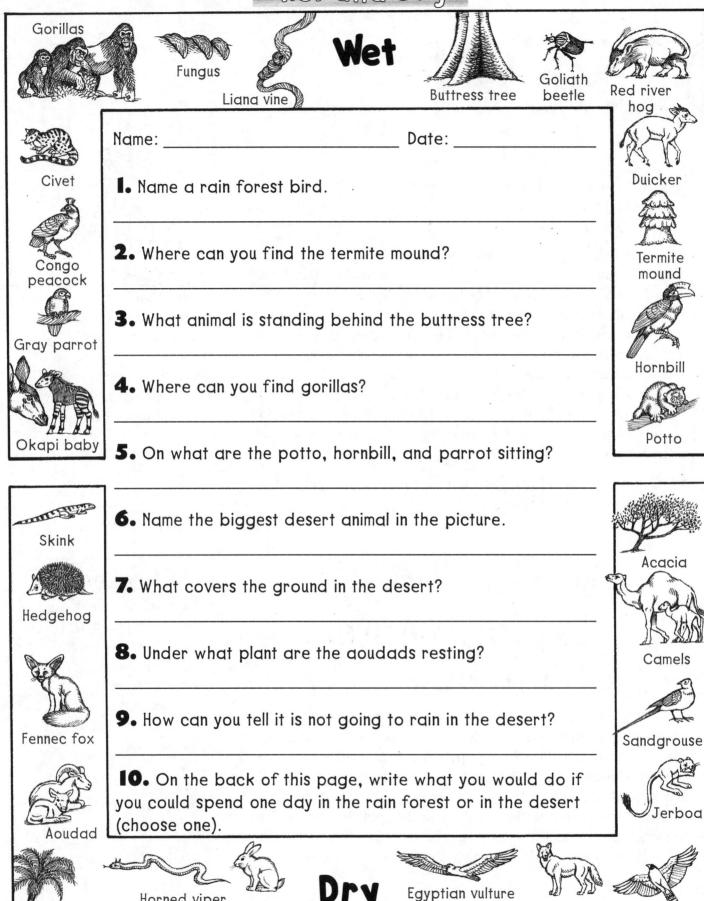

Wet

Gorillas

Fungus

Liana vine

Buttress tree

Goliath beetle

Red river hog

Civet

Congo peacock

Gray parrot

Okapi baby

Duicker

Termite mound

Hornbill

Potto

Name: _____   Date: _____

1. Name a rain forest bird.

_____

2. Where can you find the termite mound?

_____

3. What animal is standing behind the buttress tree?

_____

4. Where can you find gorillas?

_____

5. On what are the potto, hornbill, and parrot sitting?

_____

6. Name the biggest desert animal in the picture.

_____

7. What covers the ground in the desert?

_____

8. Under what plant are the aoudads resting?

_____

9. How can you tell it is not going to rain in the desert?

_____

10. On the back of this page, write what you would do if you could spend one day in the rain forest or in the desert (choose one).

Skink

Hedgehog

Fennec fox

Aoudad

Acacia

Camels

Sandgrouse

Jerboa

Palm

Horned viper

Hare

Dry

Egyptian vulture

Golden jackal

Lanner falcon

Wet and Dry

Wet

Dry

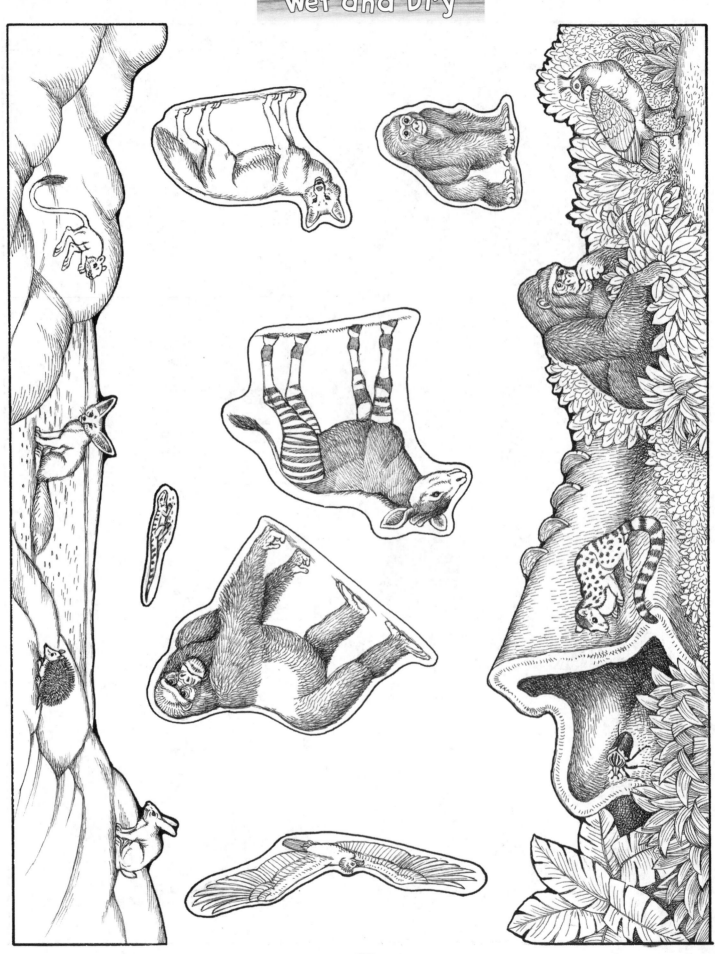

POLAR REGIONS
Far North and Far South

Teaching with the Diorama

1. Bring in a globe to show students. Point out your city or town to give students reference. Then, start at the equator and move your finger directly north to the top of the globe. Ask students, "What lies at the far north of the Earth?" *(The Arctic)* "Do you think it's cold or hot up there?" *(Cold)* "Why do you think so?" Repeat for the bottom of the globe and the far south.

2. Invite students to assemble their Far North and Far South dioramas. (See page 4.)

3. Have students take a close look at the animals on both sides of the diorama. Ask, "What do you think help these animals survive the cold?" *(Some animals have thick coats of fur or feathers. Others have thick layers of fat, called blubber, that keep them warm.)* Explain that most of the polar animals are

SCIENCE BACKGROUND

At the top of the Earth lies the Arctic Ocean, covered mostly with sheets of floating ice. At the opposite end is Antarctica, a glacier-covered continent surrounded by water. The Arctic and Antarctica are also known as the *polar regions*. These regions receive less heat from the sun than other parts of Earth. For this reason they are bitterly cold in winter when the sun never shines, and still quite cold in summer when the sun never sets.

Even though temperatures are near freezing, polar waters are rich in fish, crabs, squid, and tiny shrimp that bears, seals, and penguins hunt. Many fish in the polar regions have special substances in their blood that act like antifreeze and keep their body fluid liquid, even at temperatures below water's freezing point.

Book Links

Arctic and Antarctic
by Barbara Taylor
(Dorling Kindersley, 2000)

Greetings from Antarctica
by Sara Wheeler
(NTC Publishing, 1999)

*Over the Top of the World:
Explorer Will Steger's Trek
Across the Arctic*
by Will Steger and Jon
Bowermaster
(Scholastic, 1999)

Answers

1. No
2. Floating ice
3. Beluga or narwhal
4. Killer whale
5. Walrus
6. Narwhal
7. In the far south
8. In the far north
9. Squid and fish
10. Answers will vary, but may include: Both are very cold in winter; both have ice; both have water; whales, seals, and birds live in both places.

warm-blooded mammals and birds. These animals generate their own body heat to keep them warm even in cold weather.

4. You may want to point out two interesting animals in the Far North side of the diorama. The narwhal, a small whale with a long, spiral tusk that is actually an elongated tooth, may have inspired legends of unicorns. The Arctic tern is a hardy bird that lives in the Arctic during the summer months, then flies more than 20,000 miles to the Antarctic, where summer is just beginning. It returns in spring to the Arctic where it breeds. Invite students to draw an Arctic tern on the Far South dioramas.

5. Challenge students to use their dioramas to answer the questions on page 57.

Explore More!

How well can blubber block the cold?

How well can blubber block the cold? Make a blubber mitt to find out. Spoon about 2 cups of vegetable shortening (blubber) into a zip-lock bag. Turn another zip-lock bag inside out, then slip it into the other bag. Zip the bags closed together so that the blubber is sandwiched in-between. Make an empty mitt by slipping one plastic bag inside another. Have a volunteer place one fist into the empty mitt and the other into the blubber mitt. Have the student dip both mitts into a large bowl half-filled with ice and water for 30 seconds. Which mitt kept the hand warmer? Challenge students to think of other "chill blockers" that they can test in ice water.

Far North

Polar bears

Arctic tern

Walrus

Narwhal

Herring gull

Harp seal baby

Ringed seal

Arctic fox

Brown skua

Beluga whale

Name: _____ Date: _____

1. Are there any trees in the far south?

_____

2. What is the polar bear standing on?

_____

3. Name a whale that lives in the far north.

_____

4. Name a whale that lives in the far south.

_____

5. Which animal has two tusks?

_____

6. Which animal has one tusk?

_____

7. Where do penguins live?

_____

8. Where do polar bears live?

_____

9. What are the penguins hunting?

_____

10. How are the far north and far south alike?
On the back of this page, write your answers.

Killer whales

Adelie penguin

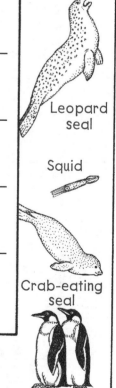

Leopard seal

Squid

Crab-eating seal

Elephant seal

Creche of emperor babies

Far South

Emperor penguins

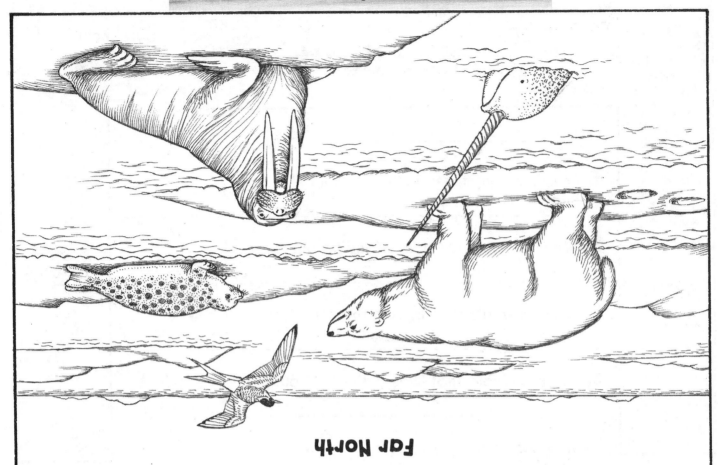

Far North

Far South

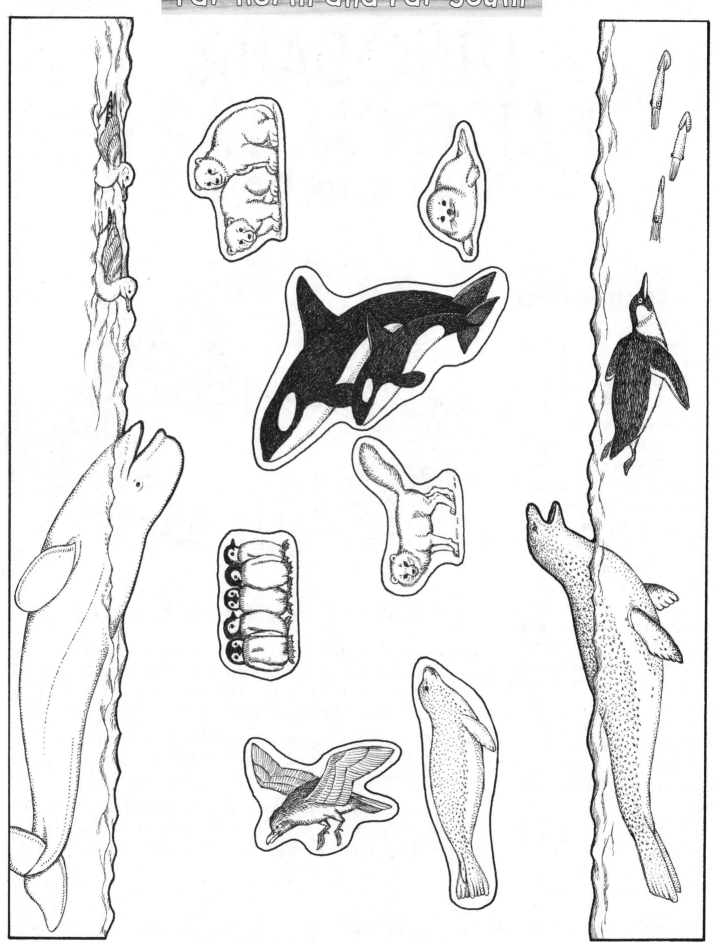

DINOSAUR NATIONAL PARK
Then and Now

Dinosaurs roamed the Earth from about 245 million years to 65 million years ago, when they became extinct. Dinosaurs were reptiles—the group that includes snakes, lizards, turtles, and alligators. New evidence shows that dinosaurs may also have been related to birds.

We know about dinosaurs from the *fossils,* or preserved remains, they left behind. When some dinosaurs died, their bodies were covered with layers of mud. Their soft body parts, such as skin and organs, decayed. Minerals in the water seeped into the hard bones and teeth, however, slowly changing them into rock-hard fossils.

Teaching with the Diorama

1. Find out what students know about dinosaurs. Ask questions, such as, "When do you think dinosaurs lived? Where? What size were they? What did they eat? What happened to them?" Challenge students to draw a picture of a dinosaur.

2. Invite students to assemble their Then and Now dioramas, which show land that is now part of Dinosaur National Park in eastern Utah and western Colorado. (See page 4.)

3. Explain to students that one side of the diorama shows the land as it looks now. The other side shows what it might have looked like about 150 million years ago. Ask, "Aside from the

animals, what else is different between the Then and Now dioramas?" *(There were more plants then; the land is drier and looks like a desert now.)*

4. Have students turn to the Then side of the diorama. Point out the different dinosaurs and their sizes. Explain that some dinosaurs were only as small as chickens, but many were huge. Help students locate the *Apatosaurus* in the diorama. This long-necked dinosaur grew up to 70 feet long and ate plants. The *Allosaurus*, on the other hand, grew up to 39 feet long, stood about 15 feet tall, and attacked other dinosaurs with its powerful jaws lined with long, sharp teeth.

5. Challenge students to use their dioramas to answer the questions on page 62.

Explore More!

How can you make your own fossils?

Make your own fossils in the classroom. Cut out pieces of sponge into bone shapes and lay them in a shallow baking pan. Cover the "bones" with a thin layer of sand. Dissolve 1/2 cup of Epsom salts into 1 cup of warm water. Pour the salt water over the sand and leave the pan in a warm, dry place for a few days. When the sand has dried out, dig up the bones. How did they change? How is this similar to how fossils are made?

Answers

1. Answers will vary.
2. Desert bighorn, mule deer, pronghorn
3. Prickly pear cactus, grass
4. Fern, cycad, conifer
5. Dinosaur bones
6. Barosaurus, Apatosaurus, Diplodocus, Brachiosaurus
7. Collared lizard
8. Answers will vary.
9. Answers will vary.
10. Answers will vary.

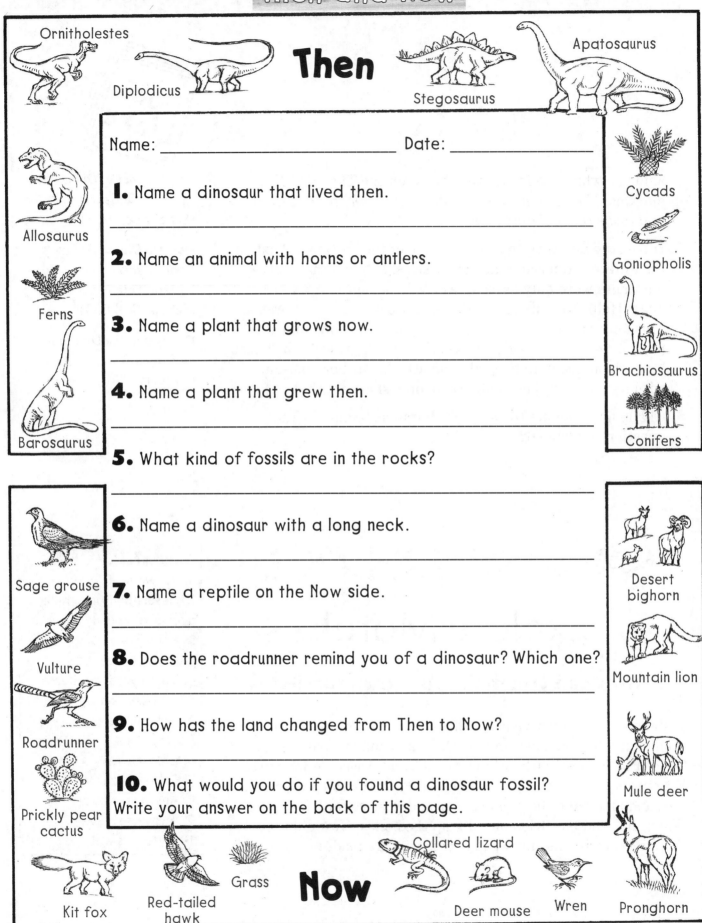

Ornitholestes

Diplodicus

Then

Stegosaurus

Apatosaurus

Allosaurus

Ferns

Barosaurus

Cycads

Goniopholis

Brachiosaurus

Conifers

Name: _____ Date: _____

1. Name a dinosaur that lived then.
_____

2. Name an animal with horns or antlers.
_____

3. Name a plant that grows now.
_____

4. Name a plant that grew then.
_____

5. What kind of fossils are in the rocks?
_____

6. Name a dinosaur with a long neck.
_____

7. Name a reptile on the Now side.
_____

8. Does the roadrunner remind you of a dinosaur? Which one?
_____

9. How has the land changed from Then to Now?
_____

10. What would you do if you found a dinosaur fossil?
Write your answer on the back of this page.

Sage grouse

Vulture

Roadrunner

Prickly pear
cactus

Desert
bighorn

Mountain lion

Mule deer

Kit fox

Red-tailed
hawk

Grass

Now

Collared lizard

Deer mouse

Wren

Pronghorn

Then

Now

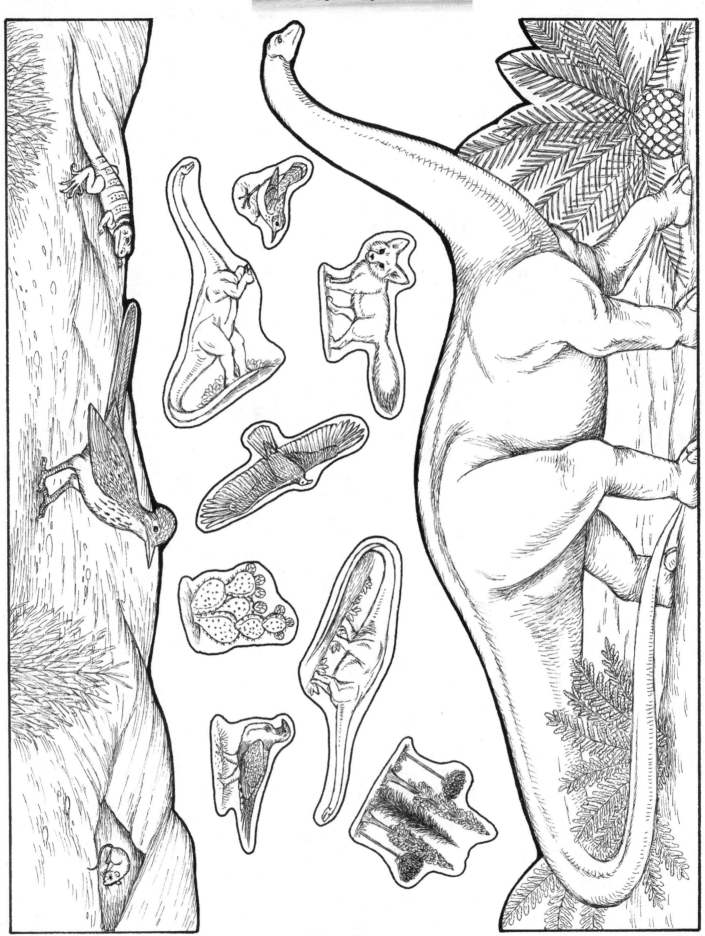